SPELLING WEEKLY PRACTICE FOR 4TH GRADE

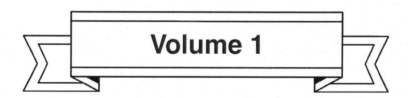

Volume 1

Scholastic Panda Education

ISBN: 978-1-953149-46-6

This Book Belongs To:

HELLO!

We are so excited to learn 4th grade spelling words together!

- **Inside you'll find 25 weeks of fun spelling units**
- **Each unit has 4 pages of exercises to practice**

Remember to:

- Look at each spelling word
- Say the word out loud
- Write the word out (sometimes in cursive!)
- Color each of the fun doodles
- Have tons of fun!

PARENTS & TEACHERS!

Free **Supplemental Document** & Answer Key

Enhance your child's learning journey with our special companion document, filled with spelling words from this workbook.

- **Reinforcement of Spelling Skills:** Regular practice with these activities can help reinforce the spelling rules learned in this workbook.
- **Comprehension Improvement:** Our fill-in-the-blank exercises and Spelling Bee/Test Practice exercises improve word understanding and comprehension skills.
- **Listening Skills Development:** Spelling Dictation exercises offer a chance to develop listening skills, further enhancing your child's/student's language proficiency.
- **Boosts Confidence:** Regular practice with these exercises can build your child's/student's confidence in their spelling ability, which can benefit all areas of their learning.
- **Flexible Learning:** These exercises can be used in the classroom or at home, offering flexible learning opportunities.

Scan the QR Code to get your free printable copies.

Includes Audio!

SCAN ME

https://bit.ly/4th-grade-dictation-swp

A READ & SPELL
B COPY & SPELL
C COVER & SPELL

1. rolled
2. finger
3. except
4. speed
5. couldn't
6. eleven
7. catch
8. itself
9. stolen
10. button

MYSTERY WORDS

1. You might use me when you need to pick something up or point. What am I?
_____

2. I can be pushed or clicked, and I help in operating devices. What am I? _____

Unscramble the words and write the correct spelling on the line

Put all of the spelling words in alphabetical order

RNGIFE _____

DTNCUOL _____

LORDEL _____

CCAHT _____

BUTOTN _____

SEDEP _____

SLNOTE _____

PETECX _____

LEEVNE _____

LFSIET _____

1. _____

2. _____

3. _____

4. _____

5. _____

6. _____

7. _____

8. _____

9. _____

10. _____

Complete the crossword puzzle with two of this week's spelling words that have a common letter. Then, rewrite those words again below in your best _cursive_ writing!

COLOR IN THE CIRCLES YOU NEED TO SPELL EACH WORD IN THE BOX.
UNSCRAMBLE THE LEFTOVER CIRCLES TO SPELL A WORD FROM THIS WEEK.

speed   stolen   itself   rolled   eleven   catch

Write the hidden word here:

_____

Which spelling word is most difficult?
Write it in a sentence to help you remember!

_____

_____

Fill in the blanks using the words below.
You will not use all of the words.

~~button~~   ~~catch~~   eleven   speed   ~~rolled~~

~~stolen~~   itself   ~~couldn't~~   ~~except~~   ~~finger~~

1. Use your __Finger__ to check the water temperature. ✓

2. It is not safe to drive faster than the __speed__ limit. ✓

3. I __couldn't__ reach the top shelf, so I asked for help. ✓

4. Whatever you do, do not press this __button__! ✓

5. I hope I do not __catch__ a cold this winter.

6. My younger sister just turned __eleven__ years old. ✓

7. A famous painting was __stolen__ from the museum.

8. Anyone can play in the ball pit __except__ adults. ✓

Start at any letter and move around the circle to find one of the spelling words.
Circle the first letter then write the full word below

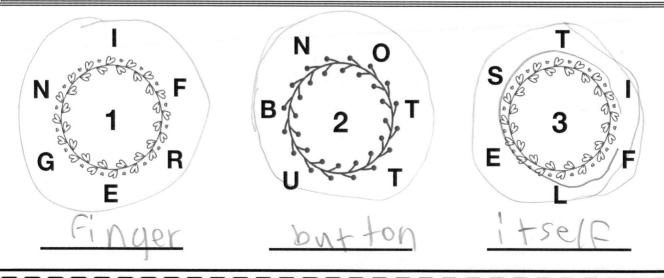

__Finger__   __button__   __itself__

Week 2

1. yourself

2. maybe

3. veteran

4. complete

5. rather

6. crowd

7. since

8. fresh

9. piece

10. cotton

MYSTERY WORDS

1. I am where people gather, especially for events or celebrations. What am I? _____

2. I'm a soft, fluffy staple fiber that grows in a boll. I'm also commonly used in making fabrics. What am I? _____

Circle each spelling word in the word search. Write each word twice in the blank spaces below as you find it.

Q	H	S	E	R	F	C	L	F	W	C	A
S	H	R	E	H	T	A	R	F	S	O	Z
B	S	B	F	M	Q	E	B	Y	A	M	R
N	V	D	L	E	K	D	U	V	R	P	Z
A	E	I	E	Y	E	Q	G	G	H	L	U
F	T	C	S	H	B	Q	N	U	B	E	R
P	E	R	R	V	R	H	B	J	J	T	K
V	R	O	U	C	O	T	T	O	N	E	L
M	A	W	O	V	X	E	C	E	I	P	E
S	N	D	Y	D	K	G	H	W	W	U	V
U	H	S	I	N	C	E	H	S	M	G	M
J	U	P	M	U	A	S	X	M	P	Z	E

1 _____ _____

2 _____ _____

3 _____ _____

4 _____ _____

5 _____ _____

6 _____ _____

7 _____ _____

8 _____ _____

9 _____ _____

10 _____ _____

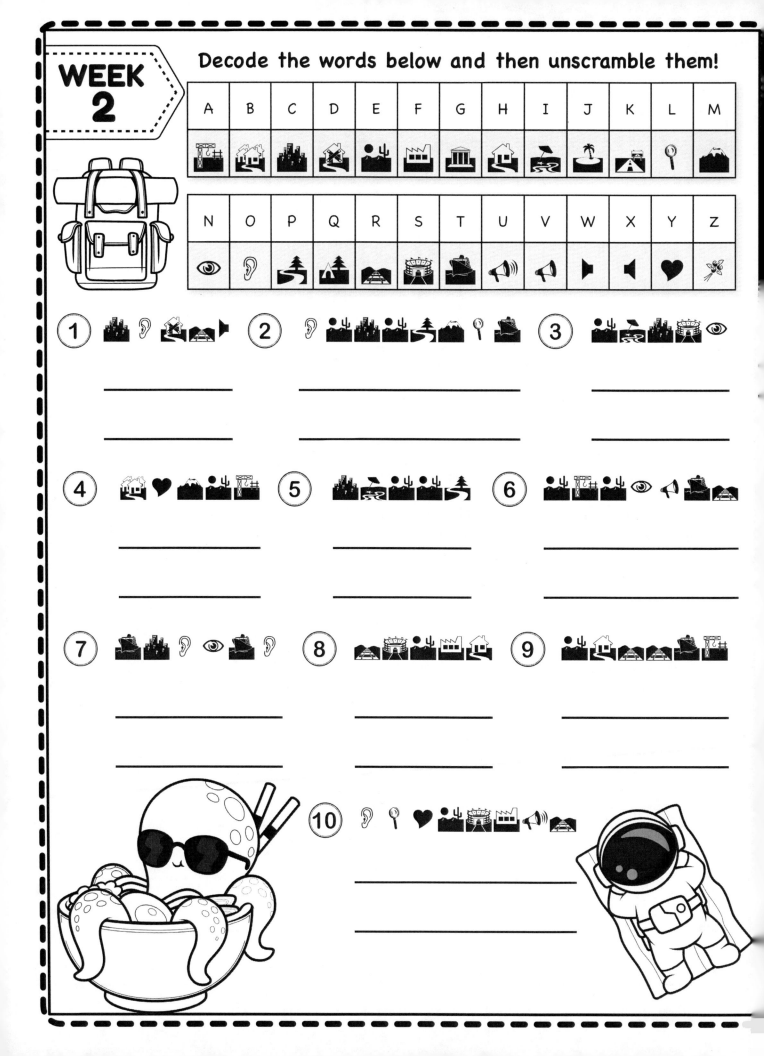

WEEK 2

Decode the words below and then unscramble them!

A	B	C	D	E	F	G	H	I	J	K	L	M

N	O	P	Q	R	S	T	U	V	W	X	Y	Z

1

2

3

4

5

6

7

8

9

10

Week 3

1. usually
2. character
3. friend
4. whom
5. heard
6. order
7. villain
8. basin
9. carton
10. become

MYSTERY WORDS

1. I am a word that means a change or transformation. What am I? _____

2. I am something you've done with your ears when someone is speaking. What am I? _____

Use the clues below to help you fill in the rest of the puzzle with this week's spelling words.

ACROSS

3. Often holds water

_____

4. Something that normally happens

_____

6. Begin to be

_____

9. She is my best _____.

_____

10. To _____ does this belong?

_____

DOWN

1. She is the main _____ in the story.

_____

2. The opposite of a hero

_____

5. The past tense of hear

_____

7. Tell someone to do something

_____

8. A box or container

_____

Choose 5 spelling words then write a short story <u>in cursive or in print</u> using all the words. Check your grammar and punctuation. Be creative and have fun!

_____

_____

_____

_____

_____

_____

_____

_____

FUN WITH MNEMONICS!

1. Create a unique phrase for each spelling word below.
2. Every new word in the phrase will start with each letter of the spelling words below.
3. Use this phrase to remember how to spell the word.
4. Write a sentence using your mnemonic to help it stick.

Ex. Basin 1. Create a mnemonic: "**B**ats **A**lways **S**leep **I**n **N**ight".
   2. Remember "basin" by recalling the phrase.
   3. Write the sentence: "To remember how to spell 'basin', I think of 'Bats Always Sleep In Night'."

1. character _____

_____

2. become _____

_____

3. villain _____

_____

4. usually _____

_____

Fill in the blanks using the words below.
You will not use all of the words.

friend	heard	basin	whom	villain
order	become	carton	character	usually

1. The milk is stored in a _____.

2. Please follow the teacher's _____.

3. To _____ did you lend your book?

4. She washed her hands in the _____.

5. The movie's _____ stole from the bank.

6. I _____ a strange noise coming from the attic.

7. The main _____ in the story is brave and kind.

8. With hard work and determination, he will _____ successful.

---

1. Write three words or phrases that come to mind for each word.
2. Focus on related words, synonyms, or words with similar feelings or concepts.
3. Be creative and think freely.
4. Remember, there are no right or wrong answers.

Ex. adventure _____discovery_____ _____explore_____ _____unknown_____

1. order _____ _____ _____

2. friend _____ _____ _____

3. character _____ _____ _____

4. basin _____ _____ _____

Week 4

A READ & SPELL

1. twelve
2. proverb
3. across
4. today
5. during
6. metaphor
7. simile
8. quiz
9. pupil
10. proposal

B COPY & SPELL / C COVER & SPELL

☑
☐ _____ _____
☐ _____ _____
☐ _____ _____
☐ _____ _____
☐ _____ _____
☐ _____ _____
☐ _____ _____
☐ _____ _____
☐ _____ _____

MYSTERY WORDS

1. I am a figure of speech, not taken literally. I paint a picture in your mind by comparing two unrelated things without using "like" or "as". What am I? _____

2. I'm a plan or suggestion. I might be used to ask someone to marry them. What am I? _____

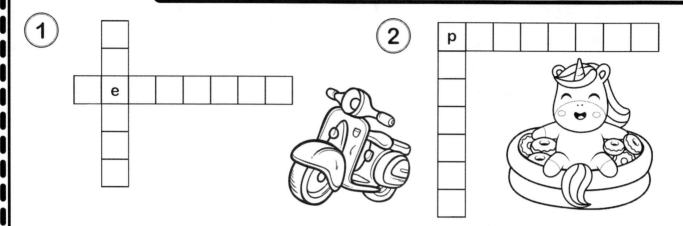

WEEK 4

Complete the crossword puzzle with two of this week's spelling words that have a common letter. Then, rewrite those words again below in your best <u>cursive</u> writing!

① **e**

② **p**

③ **a**

④ **i**

Write a SYNONYM for each word below

1. twelve _____

2. proverb _____

3. across _____

4. today _____

5. during _____

6. simile _____

7. quiz _____

Write an ANTONYM for each word below

1. proposal _____

2. pupil _____

3. quiz _____

4. during _____

5. today _____

6. metaphor _____

COLOR IN THE CIRCLES YOU NEED TO SPELL EACH WORD IN THE BOX. UNSCRAMBLE THE LEFTOVER CIRCLES TO SPELL A WORD FROM THIS WEEK.

| proposal | pupil | twelve | during | simile | quiz | proverb |

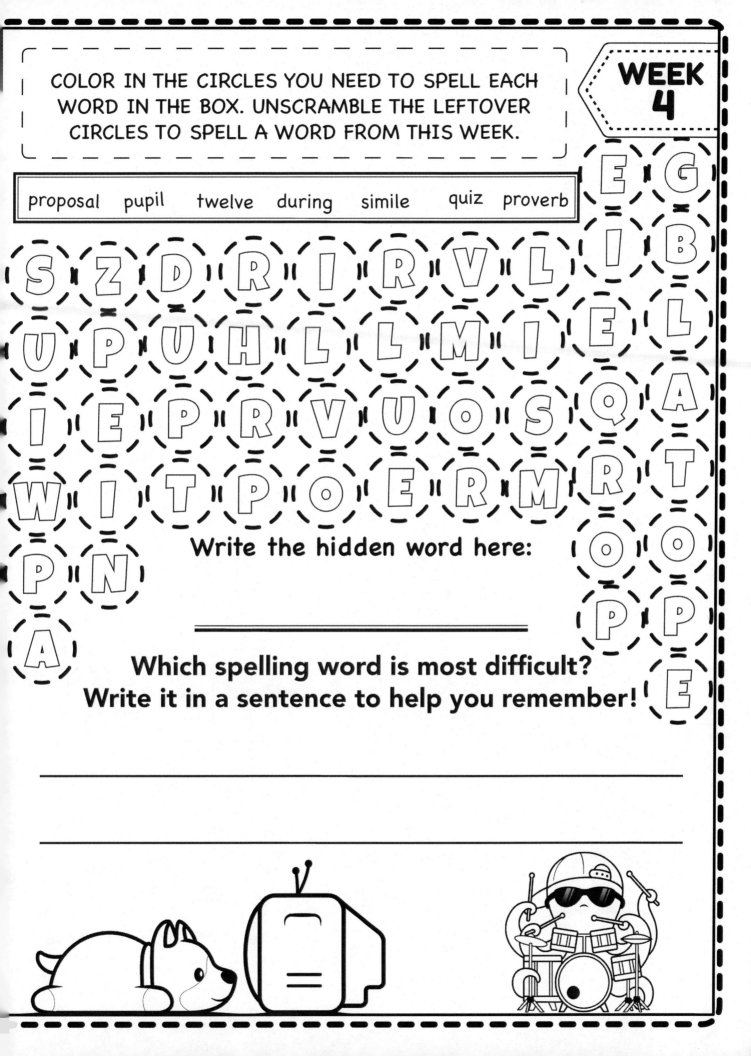

Write the hidden word here:

_____

Which spelling word is most difficult?
Write it in a sentence to help you remember!

_____

_____

Circle the correctly spelled words.
Then rewrite the incorrect words on the lines to the right.

proverb	across	today
simelie	metephor	during
quis	pupul	proposal

① _____

② _____

③ _____

④ _____

Look at the letters in the shapes and then answer the questions below.

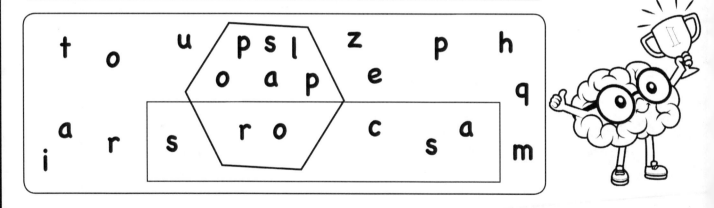

1. What word can you make with the letters in the rectangle?

_____

2. What word can you make with the letters in the hexagon?

_____

3. What two words can you make with the letters outside both shapes?

_____ _____

Week 5

1. stencil
2. twenty
3. tranquil
4. happened
5. whine
6. fossil
7. remember
8. early
9. utensil
10. mortal

MYSTERY WORDS

1. I am something very old. I was once living but now I'm turned into stone, offering clues about life millions of years ago. What am I? _____
2. I am a feeling, peaceful and calm. Like a quiet lake or a gentle breeze. What am I? _____

WEEK 5

| remember | utensil | tranquil | whine | mortal |
| happened | fossil | early | twenty | stencil |

1. Can you hand me the _____? I need it for my art project.

2. The park was so _____ early in the morning; it was a perfect time for a jog.

3. We could not believe what _____ at the surprise party last night.

4. Please don't _____. It's not going to make things better.

5. At the museum, we saw a dinosaur _____ that was millions of years old.

6. You must _____ to pack your homework in your backpack tonight.

7. We like to get to school _____ to chat with friends before class starts.

8. The chef carefully selected the _____ for his gourmet recipe.

> For each group of words below, choose a spelling word
> from this week that best fits in the same category.

1 knife, fork, spoon   _____

2 human, finite, death   _____

3 quiet, calm, peaceful   _____

4 five, ten, fifteen   _____

5 complain, moan, grumble   _____

6 occurred, transpired, unfolded   _____

7 brush, pen, marker   _____

8 prehistoric, ancient, archaic   _____

9 recall, recollect, reminisce   _____

10 morning, sunrise, dawn   _____

Circle each spelling word in the word search. Write each word twice in the blank spaces below as you find it.

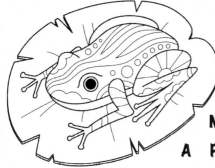

```
            F Y
          L J F X
        B V X P U K
      N N E N I H W F
    A F T D T L Y D R E
    L L I S N E T U K K Y P
    S Z L O G I H F Z W M L M Z
  J Y L H J P P P F S D H I P T H
  T P U A L A O O Q T K Z Y S Z W S A
T Q R D U W P P C I F O O Y S F E S A V
L A T R O M T R P K I Y B T O M N F B A
I M D A C K E L E T A N X F F T Y T
  C Z T T P B I Z N Z E C N J Y V
  N I J L M U G Y E Y A B E Y
    E V W E Q P C V D H I E
    T F M N F N S H Q U
    S E A R L Y P F
    R R B C U L
    T U C O
    Z U
```

1 _____ _____   6 _____ _____

2 _____ _____   7 _____ _____

3 _____ _____   8 _____ _____

4 _____ _____   9 _____ _____

5 _____ _____   10 _____ _____

MASTERING DEFINITIONS THROUGH CURSIVE PRACTICE

Trace over each definition, then write it again below in cursive. Lastly, match each word with its correct definition by writing the word in cursive next to it.

remember   utensil   tranquil   whine   mortal
happened   fossil   early   twenty   stencil

1. _____   near the beginning of a period of time

- -

2. _____   free from agitation of mind or spirit

- -

3. _____   preserved from a past geologic age

- -

4. _____   to bring to mind or think of again

- -

5. _____   a useful tool used in a household, especially in a kitchen

- -

FUN WITH MNEMONICS!

1. Create a unique phrase for each spelling word below.
2. Every new word in the phrase will start with each letter of the spelling words below.
3. Use this phrase to remember how to spell the word.
4. Write a sentence using your mnemonic to help it stick.

Ex. Basin "Bats Always Sleep In Night".

1. stencil _____

_____

2. whine _____

_____

3. happened _____

_____

4. tranquil _____

_____

Week 6

A READ & SPELL

1. thirty

2. synonym

3. antonym

4. emotion

5. covered

6. anyone

7. several

8. juvenile

9. reptile

10. toward

B COPY & SPELL

☑

☐ _____

☐ _____

☐ _____

☐ _____

☐ _____

☐ _____

☐ _____

☐ _____

☐ _____

C COVER & SPELL

_____

_____

_____

_____

_____

_____

_____

_____

_____

MYSTERY WORDS

1. I am a type of word. If you're hot, I'm cold. If you're young, I'm old. I mean the exact opposite of another word.
What am I? _____

2. I'm a way of referring to a person, but I'm not specific. I could mean you, your friend, or even someone you've never met.
What am I? _____

WEEK 6

Decode the words below and then unscramble them!

A	B	C	D	E	F	G	H	I	J	K	L	M

N	O	P	Q	R	S	T	U	V	W	X	Y	Z

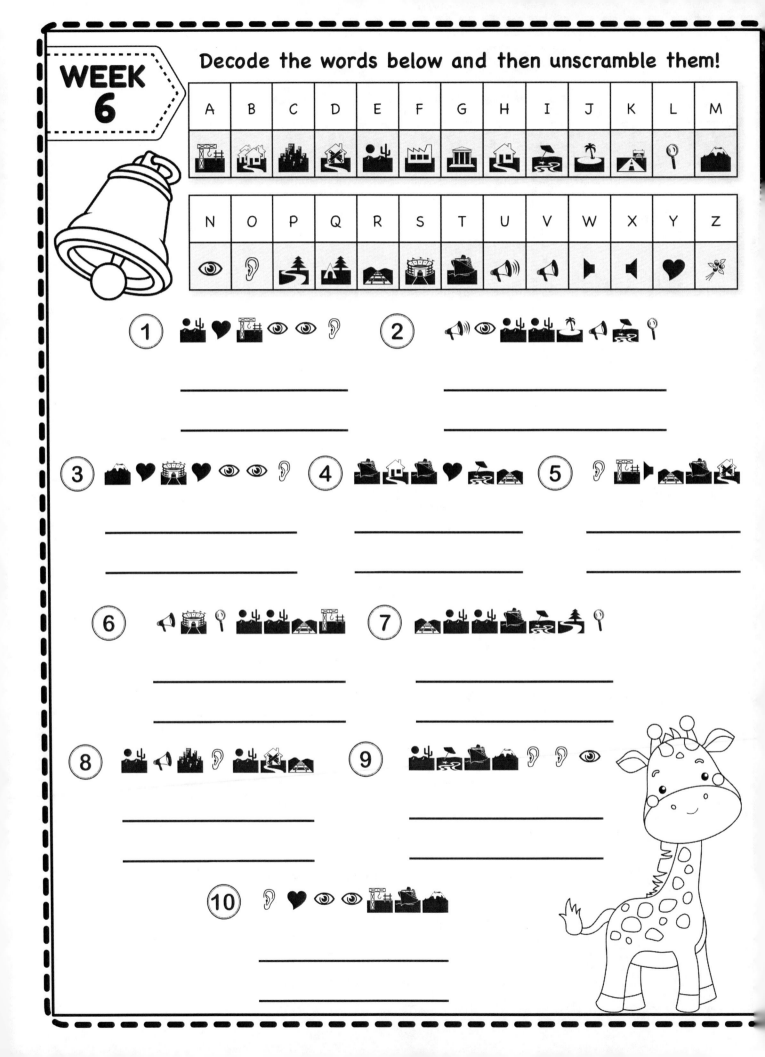

1.

2.

3.

4.

5.

6.

7.

8.

9.

10.

This diver really loves eating pizza!
1. Write the spelling words in alphabetical order on each pizza slice.
2. Have fun coloring!

Unscramble the words and write them on the lines below. Then fill in the crossword puzzle!

ACROSS

2. NENYAO _____

4. NYSOMNY _____

5. VUELJEIN _____

7. LEESAVR _____

9. RLTPIEE _____

DOWN

1. TYIRHT _____

2. NTMYOAN _____

3. ERDECOV _____

6. OTWDRA _____

8. EONIMTO _____

Week 7

A) READ & SPELL

1. bytes
2. extend
3. keyboard
4. monitor
5. vowel
6. portal
7. tunnel
8. against
9. channel
10. numerical

B) COPY & SPELL

☑

☐ _____

☐ _____

☐ _____

☐ _____

☐ _____

☐ _____

☐ _____

☐ _____

☐ _____

C) COVER & SPELL

_____

_____

_____

_____

_____

_____

_____

_____

_____

MYSTERY WORDS

1. I am used to measure the size of files on your computer. I'm a small unit of digital information. What am I? _____

2. I'm a very special kind of letter. In English, there are only five of me (sometimes six if you count 'y'). Every word has to have at least one of me. What am I? _____

**Fill in the blanks using the words below.
You will not use all of the words.**

| keyboard | portal | bytes | vowel | extend |
| tunnel | monitor | numerical | against | channel |

1. Use the _____ to type your essay for class.

2. The data file is 20 _____ too large for the disk.

3. You have to _____ your arm to reach the top shelf.

4. The _____ system is used for counting and measurement.

5. The opposing team played _____ us in the championship.

6. In the English language, every word must contain at least one _____.

7. The sci-fi show features a magical _____ that transports characters to different worlds.

8. The train travels through a long _____ to get to the other side of the mountain.

For each row of letters circle the 2nd letter, then the 4th letter, then the 6th letter, and so on. Write those circled letters on the first blank line to make a word. Now, write the letters you didn't circle on the second blank line. Finally, write both words again below, in your neatest cursive handwriting!

n k u e m y e b r o i a c r a d l

(1) _____

_____

_____

c m h o a n n i n t e o l r

(2) _____

_____

_____

a p g o a r i t n a s l t

(3) _____

_____

_____

e b x y t t e e n s d

(4) _____

_____

_____

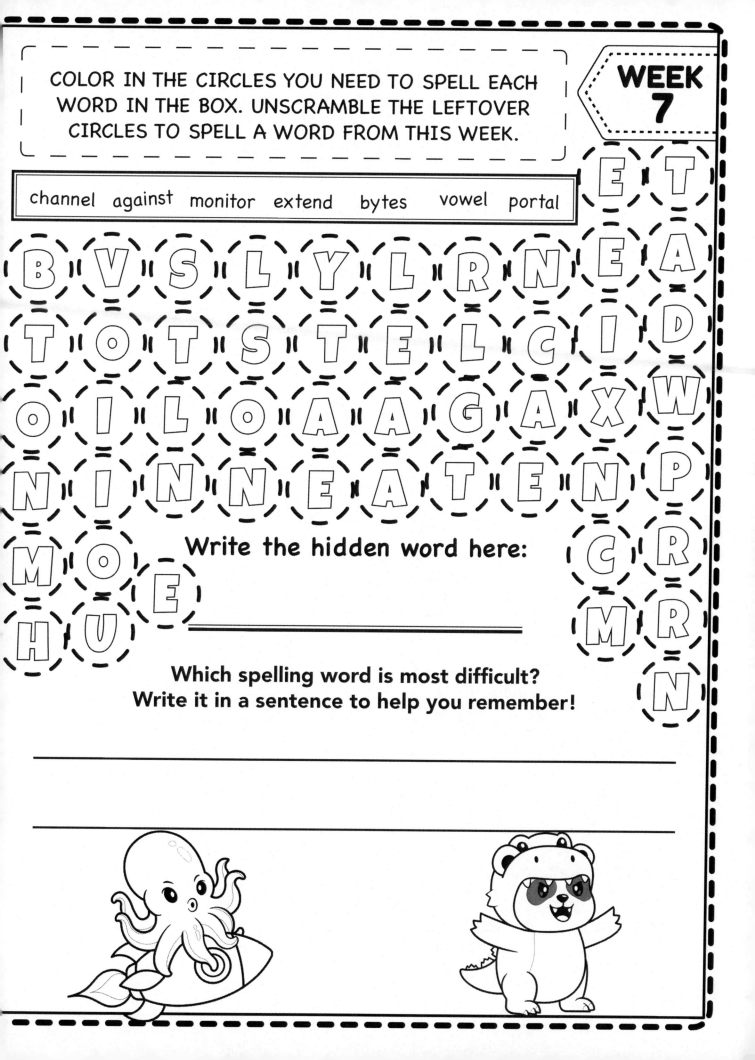

COLOR IN THE CIRCLES YOU NEED TO SPELL EACH WORD IN THE BOX. UNSCRAMBLE THE LEFTOVER CIRCLES TO SPELL A WORD FROM THIS WEEK.

WEEK 7

channel   against   monitor   extend   bytes   vowel   portal

B V S L Y L R N
T O T S T E L C
O I L O A A G A
N I N N E A T E N
M O E
H U E

E T
E A
I D
X W
N P
C R
M R
N

Write the hidden word here:

_____

**Which spelling word is most difficult?
Write it in a sentence to help you remember!**

_____

_____

Complete the crossword puzzle with two of this week's spelling words that have a common letter. Then, rewrite those words again below in your best <u>cursive</u> writing!

①

e
s

②

e

③

o

④

a

1. Write three words or phrases that come to mind for each word.
2. Focus on related words, synonyms, or words with similar feelings or concepts.
3. Be creative and think freely.
4. Remember, there are no right or wrong answers.

1. channel

2. vowel

3. numerical

4. extend

5. portal

Week 8

1. lettuce
2. spinach
3. slowly
4. squash
5. carrot
6. onion
7. jungle
8. crumble
9. cable
10. puzzle

MYSTERY WORDS

1. I'm something that can break apart or decay, especially into small pieces, if not taken care of properly. What am I? _____

2. I'm a game or toy that challenges your mind. You may need to fit pieces together, or solve a question or problem. What am I?

_____

MASTERING DEFINITIONS THROUGH CURSIVE PRACTICE

Trace over each definition, then write it again below in cursive. Lastly, match each word with its correct definition by writing the word in cursive next to it.

puzzle   crumble   onion   squash   spinach
cable   jungle   carrot   slowly   lettuce

1. _____ *a tract overgrown with thickets or masses of vegetation*

----

2. _____ *a problem or situation difficult to solve or resolve*

----

3. _____ *not quickly, fast, early, rashly, or readily*

----

4. _____ *of the lily family with pungent edible bulbs*

----

5. _____ *a wire rope or metal chain of great tensile strength*

Write a SYNONYM for each word below

1. slowly _____

2. squash _____

3. jungle _____

4. crumble _____

5. cable _____

6. puzzle _____

Write an ANTONYM for each word below

1. puzzle _____

2. crumble _____

3. jungle _____

4. slowly _____

Circle each spelling word in the word search. Write each word twice in the blank spaces below as you find it.

M	H	C	G	X	D	M	N	O	I	N	O
T	O	R	R	A	C	H	M	Y	Y	A	G
P	J	M	Y	J	C	M	L	Q	D	E	Q
M	B	W	Z	A	S	W	F	D	Z	C	P
E	M	V	N	Q	O	S	A	P	K	U	L
G	U	I	U	L	O	Z	S	O	Z	T	Y
M	P	A	S	E	L	C	A	Z	Z	T	E
S	S	W	C	R	D	M	L	Y	L	E	L
H	L	V	T	J	I	E	A	M	Y	L	B
S	G	Z	E	L	B	M	U	R	C	J	A
V	F	W	N	W	D	C	T	T	X	O	C
D	E	L	G	N	U	J	U	C	N	G	Z

1 _____ _____

2 _____ _____

3 _____ _____

4 _____ _____

5 _____

6 _____ _____

7 _____ _____

8 _____ _____

9 _____ _____

10 _____

Circle the correctly spelled words.
Then rewrite the incorrect words on the lines to the right.

puzle	cable	crumble
jungle	onoin	carrot
squash	slowlie	spineach

1 _____

2 _____

3 _____

4 _____

FUN WITH MNEMONICS!

1. Create a unique phrase for each spelling word below.
2. Every new word in the phrase will start with each letter of the spelling words below.
3. Use this phrase to remember how to spell the word.
4. Write a sentence using your mnemonic to help it stick.

Ex. Basin "Bats Always Sleep In Night".

1. crumble _____

_____

2. cable _____

_____

3. spinach _____

_____

4. squash _____

_____

Week 9

1. thirteen
2. appoint
3. discuss
4. demand
5. request
6. relief
7. structure
8. signature
9. furniture
10. departure

MYSTERY WORDS

1. This word is often used when a person is given a specific job or duty. What am I? _____

2. You do this when you're going on a vacation or even when you leave home to go to school. What am I? _____

Fill in the blanks using the words below.
You will not use all of the words.

appoint   relief   discuss   signature   thirteen
request   furniture   structure   demand   departure

1. It's necessary to _____ a meeting to plan our project.

2. Let's _____ the rules before we begin the game.

3. The teacher will _____ a student to be the class monitor.

4. After the long hike, sitting down was such a _____.

5. We need to buy some new _____ for the living room.

6. The building's _____ is very modern and eye-catching.

7. The celebrity's _____ on the poster made it more valuable.

8. Our flight's _____ time is 10:00 AM, so we should be at the airport by 8:00 AM.

For each row of letters circle the 2nd letter, then the 4th letter, then the 6th letter, and so on. Write those circled letters on the first blank line to make a word. Now, write the letters you didn't circle on the second blank line. Finally, write both words again below, in your <u>neatest cursive handwriting</u>!

r d e e l m i a e n f d

① _____
_____
_____

a d p i p s o c i u n s t s

② _____
_____
_____

t r h e i q r u t e e s e t n

③ _____
_____
_____

f s u i r g n n i a t t u u r r e e

④ _____
_____
_____

Choose 5 spelling words then write a short story <u>in cursive or in print</u> using all the words. Check your grammar and punctuation. Be creative and have fun!

_____

_____

_____

_____

_____

_____

_____

Look at the letters in the shapes and then answer the questions below

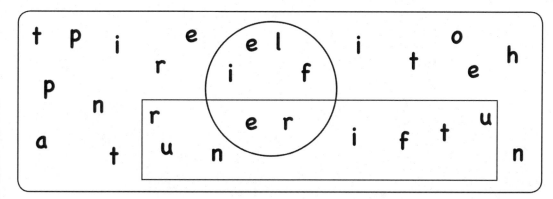

1. What word can you make with the letters in the rectangle?

   _____

2. What word can you make with the letters in the circle?

   _____

3. What two words can you make with the letters outside both shapes?

   _____   _____

Unscramble the words and write them on the lines below. Then fill in the crossword puzzle!

DOWN

1. MEDDNA _____

2. SEERTUQ _____

4. RTCURESUT _____

5. PADTRERUE _____

7. FRETUNURI _____

9. TRIHENET _____

ACROSS

3. SSUCDIS _____

6. EEILFR _____

8. NPAOTIP _____

10. IUERSNGTA _____

Week 10

1. fourteen
2. plenty
3. relax
4. bureau
5. plateau
6. field
7. clause
8. sentence
9. sketch
10. rancher

MYSTERY WORDS

1. An important place in a government or organization. What am I? _____

2. I'm part of sentences. I have a subject and a verb and express a complete thought. What am I? _____

WEEK 10

COLOR IN THE CIRCLES YOU NEED TO SPELL EACH WORD IN THE BOX. UNSCRAMBLE THE LEFTOVER CIRCLES TO SPELL A WORD FROM THIS WEEK.

| rancher | sketch | field | bureau | plenty | fourteen | relax |

Write the hidden word here:

_____

Which spelling word is most difficult?
Write it in a sentence to help you remember!

_____

_____

Help the frog with this week's spelling words.
1. Write the spelling words in alphabetical order on each pizza slice.
2. Have fun coloring!

Decode the words below and then unscramble them!

A	B	C	D	E	F	G	H	I	J	K	L	M

N	O	P	Q	R	S	T	U	V	W	X	Y	Z

1

2

3

4

5

6

7

8

9

10

Week 11

1. forty
2. English
3. split
4. half
5. minus
6. plus
7. totally
8. really
9. finally
10. locally

MYSTERY WORDS

1. I'm not far or distant, I'm much closer than you think. You'll find me in your community, no need for a long drive. What am I? _____

2. I'm not whole or complete, but instead, I've been divided. You might do this to a sandwich or a piece of wood. What am I? _____

MASTERING DEFINITIONS THROUGH CURSIVE PRACTICE

Trace over each definition, then write it again below in cursive. Lastly, match each word with its correct definition by writing the word in cursive next to it.

locally   really   plus   split   forty
finally   totally   minus   half   English

1. _____ to divide lengthwise usually along a grain or seam or by layers

---

---

2. _____ to a complete degree

---

3. _____ at the end of period of time

---

4. _____ diminished by, a negative quantity

---

5. _____ a number equal to four times 10

CATEGORY CONNECTION

For each group of words below, choose a spelling word from this week that best fits in the same category.

1. Add, increase, enhance _____

2. Spanish, French, German _____

3. Globally, internationally, nationally _____

4. Subtract, decrease, deduct _____

5. twenty five, thirty, thirty five _____

Circle each spelling word in the word search. Write each word twice in the blank spaces below as you find it.

```
            Y W
          T M O Y
        R S M C L N
      O K U J K L N B
      F N D L E F A U J I
    K J C B P B U C I V W M
    G Y L L A E R L O B Z E T V
  Y X O U Z S N J V L D U F D Z W
  Z D X M B Q Y U M L A B N X N J P F
H I Q R B L T B V N R T H N B Y J B N S
R Y G W J H E W Z J I H S I L G N E F U
  F K O X H D F M X Y M P A H Y G G O
  O N N W Z I C D O F L V M T T D
    G F C B N B G Z B I C O H T
      B P A A A O X C T T A G
        P I L I W W Y A L C
          X L S K R L F D
          Y I N L R V
            H Y Y A
            V P
```

 1 _____ _____   6 _____ _____

2 _____ _____   7 _____ _____

3 _____ _____   8 _____ _____

 4 _____ _____   9 _____ _____

5 _____ _____   10 _____ _____

WEEK 11

Complete the crossword puzzle with two of this week's spelling words that have a common letter. Then, rewrite those words again below in your best <u>cursive</u> writing!

1 (crossword grid, with letter **t**)

2 (crossword grid, with letter **i**)

3 (crossword grid, with letter **f**)

4 (crossword grid, with letter **u**)

1. Write four words or phrases that come to mind for each word.
2. Focus on related words, synonyms, or words with similar feelings or concepts.
3. Be creative and think freely.
4. Remember, there are no right or wrong answers.

1. minus _____ _____ _____ _____

2. English _____ _____ _____ _____

3. split _____ _____ _____ _____

4. locally _____ _____ _____ _____

5. forty _____ _____ _____ _____

Week 12

1. slide
2. swings
3. goal
4. coach
5. became
6. shown
7. blown
8. pasture
9. adventure
10. literature

MYSTERY WORDS

1. I am not a book, but I hold many stories. Novels, poems, and plays all fall under my umbrella. You'll learn about me in English class. What am I? _____

2. You'll find me out in the country, not in a city. I'm a wide open space, where animals might graze. What am I? _____

Unscramble the words and write them on the lines below. Then fill in the crossword puzzle!

ACROSS

2. LAGO _____

3. NSHOW _____

4. ACOHC _____

ACROSS

6. GSNSWI _____

7. AUTELEIRRT _____

8. PATEURS _____

9. CEMEBA _____

DOWN

1. NLOBW _____

3. DSILE _____

5. VDUERANET _____

This is one bad baby and he loves eating cookies!
1. Write the spelling words in alphabetical order on each cookie.
2. Have fun coloring!

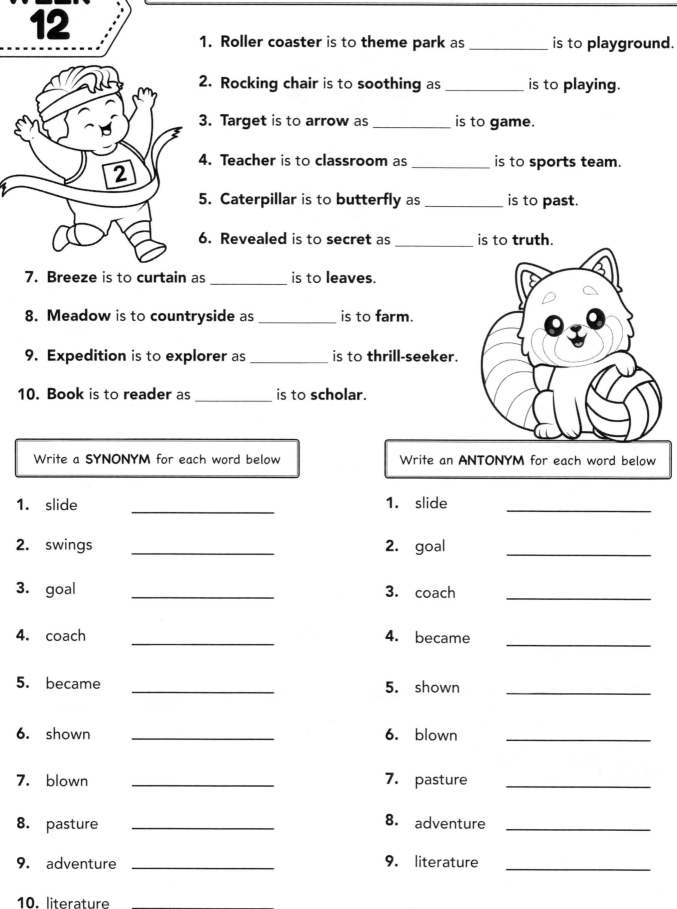

WEEK 12

Use a spelling word from this week to complete each analogy below.

1. **Roller coaster** is to **theme park** as _____ is to **playground**.

2. **Rocking chair** is to **soothing** as _____ is to **playing**.

3. **Target** is to **arrow** as _____ is to **game**.

4. **Teacher** is to **classroom** as _____ is to **sports team**.

5. **Caterpillar** is to **butterfly** as _____ is to **past**.

6. **Revealed** is to **secret** as _____ is to **truth**.

7. **Breeze** is to **curtain** as _____ is to **leaves**.

8. **Meadow** is to **countryside** as _____ is to **farm**.

9. **Expedition** is to **explorer** as _____ is to **thrill-seeker**.

10. **Book** is to **reader** as _____ is to **scholar**.

Write a **SYNONYM** for each word below

1. slide _____

2. swings _____

3. goal _____

4. coach _____

5. became _____

6. shown _____

7. blown _____

8. pasture _____

9. adventure _____

10. literature _____

Write an **ANTONYM** for each word below

1. slide _____

2. goal _____

3. coach _____

4. became _____

5. shown _____

6. blown _____

7. pasture _____

8. adventure _____

9. literature _____

Week 13

1. fifteen
2. polite
3. peanut
4. soccer
5. backpack
6. decide
7. contain
8. course
9. surface
10. produce

MYSTERY WORDS

1. I'm a word that's quite fruitful. At the grocery store, you'll find me in aisles filled with apples, oranges, and bananas. What am I? _____

2. Like a jar or a box, I can hold something inside. A secret, an item, or a rule that's applied. What am I? _____

Fill in the blanks using the words below. You will not use all of the words.

backpack	soccer	peanut	polite	fifteen
decide	contain	course	surface	produce

1. Tom forgot his _____ at home and had to go back to get it.

2. You must _____ if you want to join the art or the dance club.

3. The can of paint may _____ enough to cover the entire wall.

4. It's important to be _____ when meeting new people.

5. Sally loves to play _____ on the weekends.

6. The teacher guided us through the _____ material for the week.

7. Be careful when walking on the slippery _____.

8. Farmers have a big responsibility to _____ food for everyone.

> **Look at the letters in the shapes and then answer the questions below**

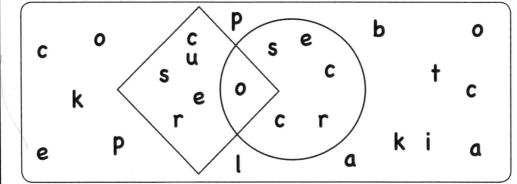

1. What word can you make with the letters in the square?

   _____

2. What word can you make with the letters in the circle?

   _____

3. What two words can you make with the letters outside both shapes?

   _____ _____

COLOR IN THE CIRCLES YOU NEED TO SPELL EACH WORD IN THE BOX. UNSCRAMBLE THE LEFTOVER CIRCLES TO SPELL A WORD FROM THIS WEEK.

contain	soccer	fifteen	decide	surface	produce	polite

C I E C E C A C C F N R O N

S O F C C D E R E E

N U I D C I I D E F I

T T E L P R O S U P

A K P C O A C

Write the hidden word here:

_____

Which spelling word is most difficult?
Write it in a sentence to help you remember!

_____

_____

Unscramble each word and write it on the first line.
Then write the word in cursive on the second line.

IEPLTO

1 _____ _____

OUCSER

2 _____ _____

ABKCCPKA

3 _____ _____

CORUEPD

4 _____ _____

AINOCNT

5 _____ _____

ROSCCE

6 _____ _____

APTUEN

7 _____ _____

EENTIFF

8 _____ _____

RCSFUEA

9 _____ _____

EEDCDI

10 _____ _____

For each row of letters circle the 2nd letter, then the 4th letter, then the 6th letter, and so on.
Write those circled letters on the first blank line to make a word. Now, write the letters you didn't circle
on the second blank line. Finally, write both words again below, in your neatest cursive handwriting!

1 p c e o a u n r u s t e

_____

_____

_____

2 p d r e o c d i u d c e e

_____

_____

_____

3 f p i o f l t i e t e e n

_____

_____

_____

4 b s a u c r k f p a a c c e k

_____

_____

_____

A READ & SPELL

1. building
2. spelling
3. erratic
4. fifty
5. receive
6. revise
7. deceive
8. scientist
9. inside
10. rupture

B COPY & SPELL

☑
☐ _____ _____
☐ _____ _____
☐ _____ _____
☐ _____ _____
☐ _____ _____
☐ _____ _____
☐ _____ _____
☐ _____ _____
☐ _____ _____

C COVER & SPELL

MYSTERY WORDS

1. Sometimes I'm calm, sometimes I'm wild, I change without reason, like a mischievous child. What am I? _____

2. I'm what happens when something breaks or bursts. I can happen to a balloon, a pipe, or even worse. What am I? _____

Complete the crossword puzzle with two of this week's spelling words that have a common letter. Then, rewrite those words again below in your best <u>cursive</u> writing!

①

l

②

e

③

i

④

e

Circle the correctly spelled words.
Then rewrite the incorrect words on the lines to the right.

revise	fifty	eratic
rupchure	recieve	spelling
inside	scientis	building

① _____

② _____

③ _____

④ _____

Circle each spelling word in the word search. Write each word twice in the blank spaces below as you find it.

R	S	U	O	F	C	P	H	M	J	H	R
A	V	P	D	E	C	E	I	V	E	L	R
T	C	Y	E	R	U	T	P	U	R	E	W
F	S	T	M	L	K	Y	R	E	C	H	B
I	Z	I	J	B	L	K	S	E	Q	U	N
F	D	C	T	G	I	I	I	J	I	C	U
T	I	K	V	N	V	V	N	L	A	I	E
Y	S	U	S	E	E	T	D	G	Y	T	C
J	T	I	R	Y	X	I	X	C	W	A	D
Q	D	C	Y	S	N	L	C	U	S	R	X
E	Y	D	B	G	H	S	T	S	W	R	E
L	T	Y	S	R	I	S	V	N	U	E	N

1 _____ _____   6 _____ _____

2 _____ _____   7 _____ _____

3 _____ _____   8 _____ _____

4 _____ _____   9 _____ _____

5 _____ _____   10 _____ _____

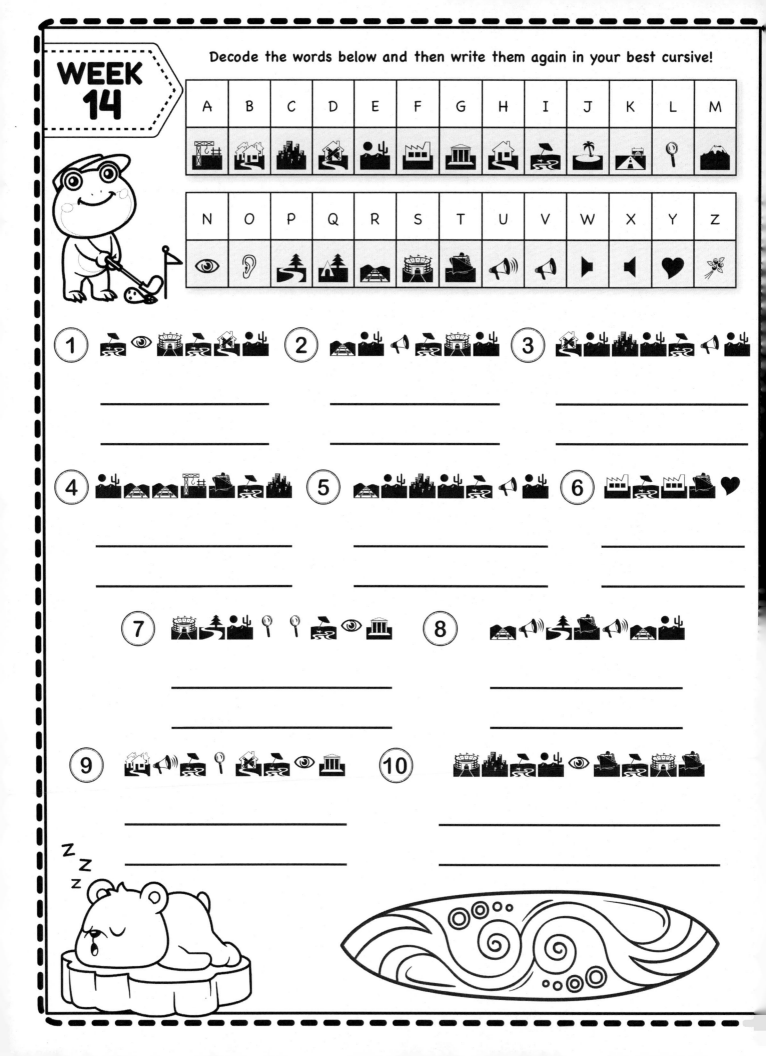

WEEK 14

Decode the words below and then write them again in your best cursive!

A	B	C	D	E	F	G	H	I	J	K	L	M

N	O	P	Q	R	S	T	U	V	W	X	Y	Z

1. _____

2. _____

3. _____

4. _____

5. _____

6. _____

7. _____

8. _____

9. _____

10. _____

Week 15

1. sixteen
2. chicken
3. elephant
4. island
5. gorilla
6. dolphin
7. machine
8. ticket
9. diet
10. puppet

B COPY & SPELL

C COVER & SPELL

MYSTERY WORDS

1. I'm big and grey, with a long trunk that I use to spray. In the jungle is where I like to play. What am I? _____

2. I'm controlled by strings, yet I can dance and sing. I come to life without a single living thing. What am I? _____

MASTERING DEFINITIONS THROUGH CURSIVE PRACTICE

Trace over each definition, then write it again below in cursive. Lastly, match each word with its correct definition by writing the word in cursive next to it.

puppet   ticket   dolphin   island   chicken
diet   machine   gorilla   elephant   sixteen

1. _____ specific food and drink regularly provided or consumed

   ----

2. _____ land surrounded by water and smaller than a continent

   ----

3. _____ a mechanically, electrically, or electronically operated device

   ----

4. _____ a document that serves as a certificate, license, or permit

   ----

5. _____ a small-scale figure (as of a person or animal) that fits over and is moved by the hand

   ----

Use a spelling word from this week to complete each analogy below.

1. **Ten** is to **twenty** as **eight** is to _____ .

2. **Duck** is to **pond** as **hen** is to _____ coop.

3. **Mouse** is to **rodent** as **Dumbo** is to _____ .

4. **House** is to **block** as **Australia** is to _____ .

5. **Monkey** is to **primate** as **King Kong** is to _____ .

6. **Fish** is to **aquatic** as **Flipper** is to _____ .

7. **Pencil** is to **tool** as **computer** is to _____ .

8. **Show** is to **performance** as **roller coaster** is to _____ .

9. **Eating** is to **feast** as **fasting** is to _____ .

10. **Doll** is to **toy** as **Pinocchio** is to _____ .

CATEGORY CONNECTION

For each group of words below, choose a spelling word
from this week that best fits in the same category.

1 computer, refrigerator, car _____

2 chimpanzee, orangutan, baboon _____

3 whale, shark, seal _____

4 fifteen, seventeen, eighteen _____

5 doll, action figure, teddy bear _____

6 exercise, nutrition, sleep _____

7 lion, tiger, zebra _____

8 receipt, invoice, voucher _____

9 turkey, duck, goose _____

10 peninsula, continent, archipelago _____

Unscramble each word and write it on the first line.
Then write the word again on the second line in your best cursive!

TEPPUP

1 _____ _____

KNCEHCI

2 _____ _____

DITE

3 _____ _____

LNIPHOD

4 _____ _____

HELATEPN

5 _____ _____

IDNLAS

6 _____ _____

ILRAGOL

7 _____ _____

TCKTEI

8 _____ _____

ENTIXSE

9 _____ _____

AINEHMC

10 _____ _____

WEEK 15

With the spelling words from this week, fill in the blanks in the story below. Some words may be used twice!

There was a lively farm filled with many animals. Among them was a _____ named Charlie, known for his bright red comb and clucky voice. One day, while pecking around the barn, Charlie found a shiny golden _____. This was no ordinary _____, it was an invitation to an amazing animal carnival on a nearby _____ in the middle of a sparkling blue sea.

Thrilled, Charlie set off for the carnival. There, he saw many fascinating animals. There was Eddie, a giant _____ known for his huge tusks and impressive tricks. He could even balance on one foot! Another performer was Daisy, a graceful _____ who did spectacular flips and leaps in a big water tank.

The most intriguing animal Charlie met was a clever _____ named Garry. Garry, with his soft black fur, was especially unique because he could solve puzzles and use sign language to communicate with people.

All the animals were incredibly fit and active, Charlie noticed. He learned that it was due to their balanced _____, which kept them healthy and strong.

Experiencing all these amazing things, Charlie felt a joy he hadn't felt since he was _____ years old. Before leaving the carnival, he noticed a _____ that made custom toys. Charlie got a toy gorilla to remember Garry and this extraordinary day.

Back at the farm, Charlie had so much to share with his friends about his unforgettable adventure.

Using as many spelling words as possible, in cursive write what you enjoyed most about Charlie's adventure. You can even write about what you think Charlie did the next day!

_____

_____

_____

_____

_____

_____

Week 16

A READ & SPELL

B COPY & SPELL

C COVER & SPELL

1. understand
2. brought
3. force
4. kangaroo
5. wolves
6. alligator
7. monkey
8. crocodile
9. system
10. sixty

MYSTERY WORDS

1. I'm made up of parts, all working together. Whether it's computers, or the weather, I'm in operation forever. What am I? _____

2. I push or I pull, I'm at work everywhere. In magnets, in wind, even gravity has me to share. What am I? _____

Circle the correctly spelled words.
Then rewrite the incorrect words on the lines to the right.

undurstand	wolves	crocodile
force	alligater	system
kangaro	monkey	sixtie

1 _____

2 _____

3 _____

4 _____

Look at the letters in the shapes and then answer the questions below

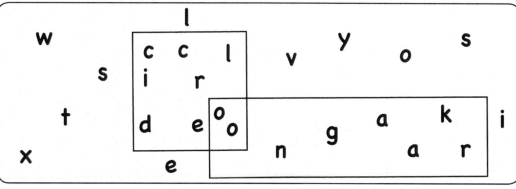

w   l   v   y   s
   s c c l   o
   t i r   a k i
      d e o o g   r
   x   e   n   a r

1. What word can you make with the letters in the square?

    _____

2. What word can you make with the letters in the rectangle?

    _____

3. What two words can you make with the letters outside both shapes?

    _____ _____

This scuba kitty is exploring underwater! Write the spelling words in alphabetical order near each of the marine life. And then have fun coloring!

WEEK
16

Use the clues below to help you fill in the rest of the puzzle with this week's spelling words.

ACROSS

3. Three times twenty

_____

5. Known to eat bananas

_____

6. Past tense of bring

_____

8. To comprehend

_____

10. Strength or power

_____

DOWN

1. Rhymes with "waiter"

_____

2. Mammal that hunts in packs

_____

4. Reptile with a long, narrow snout

_____

7. Usually found in Australia

_____

9. Also known as a process

_____

Week 17

A READ & SPELL

1. seventeen
2. browser
3. memory
4. explain
5. adage
6. courage
7. language
8. luggage
9. storage
10. thousand

B COPY & SPELL

☑
☐ _____
☐ _____
☐ _____
☐ _____
☐ _____
☐ _____
☐ _____
☐ _____
☐ _____

C COVER & SPELL

_____
_____
_____
_____
_____
_____
_____
_____
_____

MYSTERY WORDS

1. I'm packed and I'm zipped, for travel I'm fit. I carry your clothes and more, on every trip. What am I? _____

2. I'm a saying, old and wise, that your grandparents might advise. People share me far and wide, for in me, wisdom often lies. What am I? _____

Fill in the blanks using the words below.
You will not use all of the words.

| adage | explain | memory | browser | seventeen |
| courage | language | luggage | storage | thousand |

1. The _____ on my computer isn't working; I need to refresh it.

2. When we travel, we always bring too much _____.

3. Can you _____ how this game is played?

4. It takes a lot of _____ to stand up to a bully.

5. I have a good _____ for birthdays; I never forget them.

6. Learning a new _____ can be challenging but rewarding.

7. I couldn't find my toy because it was in the _____ room.

8. My teacher shared an old _____ to teach us about wisdom.

1. Write four words or phrases that come to mind for each word.
2. Focus on related words, synonyms, or words with similar feelings or concepts.
3. Be creative and think freely.
4. Remember, there are no right or wrong answers.

1. thousand _____ _____ _____ _____

2. memory _____ _____ _____ _____

3. courage _____ _____ _____ _____

4. luggage _____ _____ _____ _____

5. browser _____ _____ _____ _____

COLOR IN THE CIRCLES YOU NEED TO SPELL EACH WORD IN THE BOX. UNSCRAMBLE THE LEFTOVER CIRCLES TO SPELL A WORD FROM THIS WEEK.

| thousand | luggage | adage | memory | courage | browser |

A E G G R M N E G C M

A D O R E L O G R A A

U N S G T O Y O A G B

H R U G L W E U D A A

A A D S

U E E

Write the hidden word here:

_____

**Which spelling word is most difficult?
Write it in a sentence to help you remember!**

_____

_____

WEEK 17

1. browser _____

2. memory _____

3. explain _____

4. adage _____

5. courage _____

6. language _____

7. luggage _____

8. storage _____

1. memory _____

2. explain _____

3. courage _____

4. language _____

5. storage _____

FUN WITH MNEMONICS!

1. Create a unique phrase for each spelling word below.
2. Every new word in the phrase will start with each letter of the spelling words below.
3. Use this phrase to remember how to spell the word.
4. Write a sentence using your mnemonic to help it stick.

Ex. Basin "**B**ats **A**lways **S**leep **I**n **N**ight".

1. language _____
_____

2. courage _____
_____

3. thousand _____
_____

4. explain _____
_____

Week 18

1. wedge
2. ridge
3. bridge
4. pledge
5. filled
6. caution
7. average
8. equation
9. rhombus
10. seventy

MYSTERY WORDS

1. A promise made, a vow to keep, to do my best, a word to reap. In honor's name, my word I leave. What am I? _____

2. I'm not a square, yet four sides I bear. All sides are equal, which makes me rare. You'll find me in geometry, if you dare. What am I? _____

Decode the words below and then unscramble them!

A	B	C	D	E	F	G	H	I	J	K	L	M

N	O	P	Q	R	S	T	U	V	W	X	Y	Z

1

2

3

4

5

6

7

8

9

10

Choose 5 spelling words then write a short story <u>in cursive or in print</u> using all the words. Check your grammar and punctuation. Be creative and have fun!

_____

_____

_____

_____

_____

_____

Complete the crossword puzzle with two of this week's spelling words that have a common letter. Then, rewrite those words again below in your best <u>cursive</u> writing!

1

l

2

r

_____   _____

3

e

4

o

_____   _____

MASTERING DEFINITIONS THROUGH CURSIVE PRACTICE

Trace over each definition, then write it again below in cursive. Lastly, match each word with its correct definition by writing the word in cursive next to it.

seventy   ridge   filled   caution   equation
wedge   bridge   pledge   average   rhombus

1. _____ *prudent forethought to minimize risk*

2. _____ *a complex of variable factors*

3. _____ *to put into as much as can be held or contained*

4. _____ *a time, place, or means of connection or transition*

5. _____ *a binding promise or agreement to do or forbear*

For each row of letters circle the 2nd letter, then the 4th letter, then the 6th letter, and so on. Write those circled letters on the first blank line to make a word. Now, write the letters you didn't circle on the second blank line. Finally, write both words again below, in your <u>neatest cursive handwriting</u>!

1. s r e h v o e m n b t u y s
_____
_____
_____

2. e a q v u e a r t a i g o e n
_____
_____
_____

3. c f a i u l t l i e o d n
_____
_____
_____

4. b p r l i e d d g g e e
_____
_____
_____

Week 19

1. dragon
2. castle
3. knight
4. queen
5. prince
6. kingdom
7. alone
8. ghost
9. robot
10. program

MYSTERY WORDS

1. I am filled with knights and kings, a land of fairy tales where imagination takes wings. What am I? _____

2. I can breathe fire, and in fairy tales, I am a flier. I guard treasure with might, always a fearsome sight. What am I? _____

WEEK 19

This chili's mouth is on fire, help it get some milk!
1. Write the spelling words in alphabetical order on each milk carton.
2. Have fun coloring!

Circle each spelling word in the word search. Write each word twice in the blank spaces below as you find it.

```
D J U D                        K C X W
Z C F E G                      P N Y A I
G I H N X R                    Y E I A F I
V O U M C A T                  Z E Z G P F D
  X P X G P U B              D U B R H V A
    J E E Q L U M          R Q D W F T I
    J I O K O X S Z H F P R X C
    N M I G H O S T E C O W
    G N L S N O G A R D
    G R Z B S W F L
    D L O D H T M B
    X O R B P K L Y U Z
  U T M P R O G R A M Y Q
  B E T K I M Q O M I N C N V
N G P R N A T        M E T T U U E
  Q G L S C A E      R L G M W Q T
K Z J S E L T        C T Q T C P D
W J X N O O          W S Y F Q C
X B T N G            J A J S S
S I E W              Y C J K
```

1 _____ _____

2 _____ _____

3 _____ _____

4 _____ _____

5 _____ _____

6 _____ _____

7 _____ _____

8 _____ _____

9 _____ _____

10 _____ _____

Complete the crossword puzzle with two of this week's spelling words that have a common letter. Then, rewrite those words again below in your best _cursive_ writing!

1 a

2 a

3 k

4 r o

Circle the correctly spelled words.
Then rewrite the incorrect words on the lines to the right.

goste	dragon	knight
cassle	prince	kingdum
program	queene	alone

1 _____

2 _____

3 _____

4 _____

Week 20

1. solo
2. duet
3. cello
4. special
5. heavy
6. trio
7. choir
8. remote
9. include
10. homework

MYSTERY WORDS

1. You use me when you want to make sure nothing is left out. I'm often used when giving instructions or making a list. What am I? _____

2. Not ordinary or usual, I stand out from the rest. I'm not the same, I'm considered the best. What am I? _____

First, unscramble each word, then write it neatly in cursive on the next line. Finally, fill those words into the crossword puzzle!

DOWN

2. ETMROE _____

3. OLOS _____

4. ELASCPI _____

6. AYEVH _____

8. LECOL _____

9. TEUD _____

ACROSS

1. HCRIO _____

5. MOROHKEW _____

7. NUDLIEC _____

10. ROIT _____

COLOR IN THE CIRCLES YOU NEED TO SPELL EACH WORD IN THE BOX. UNSCRAMBLE THE LEFTOVER CIRCLES TO SPELL A WORD FROM THIS WEEK.

solo   duet   cello   heavy   remote   include   special

C L I A H O V O D Y

E U T E O R V E C L

H E D E R E U S P K

L S L O O M O A E E

L C N T

I W

M

Write the hidden word here:

_____

Which spelling word is most difficult?
Write it in a sentence to help you remember!

_____

_____

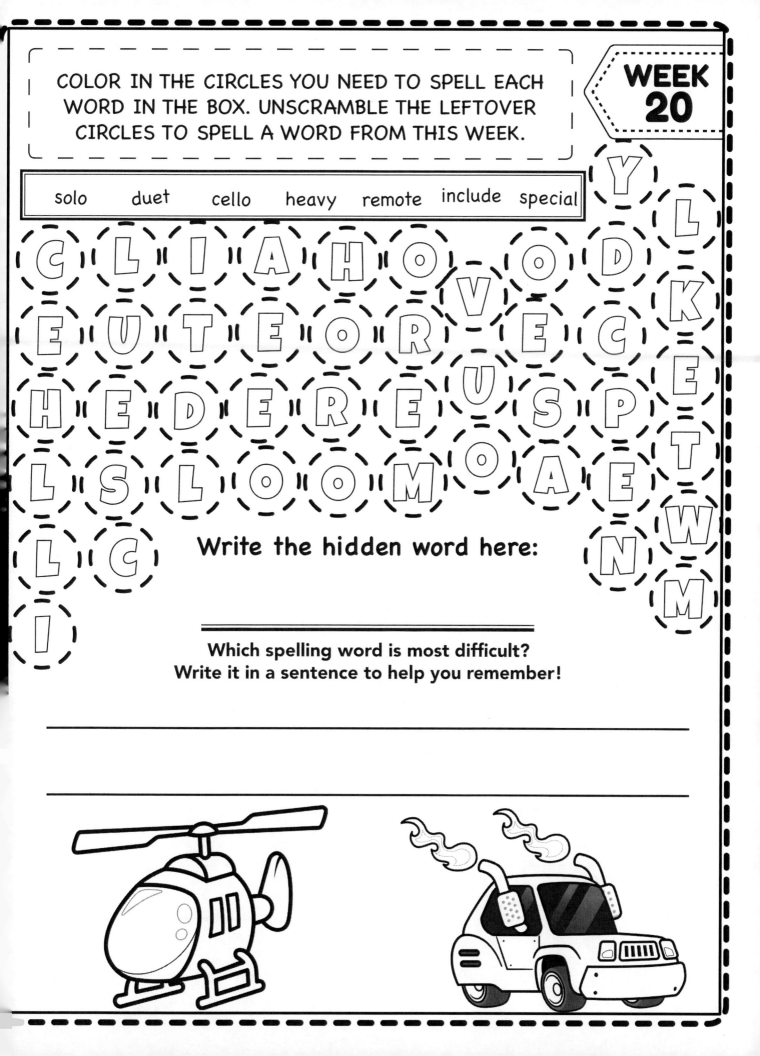

WEEK 20

Trace over each definition, then write it again below in cursive. Lastly, match each word with its correct definition by writing the word in cursive next to it.

homework   remote   trio   special   duet
include   choir   heavy   cello   solo

1. _____ far removed in space, time, or relation

----

2. _____ a group or set of three

----

3. _____ an assignment given to a student outside of class

----

4. _____ having great weight

----

5. _____ a bass member of the violin family tuned an octave below the viola

----

----

1. Write four words or phrases that come to mind for each word.
2. Focus on related words, synonyms, or words with similar feelings or concepts.
3. Be creative and think freely.
4. Remember, there are no right or wrong answers.

1. remote _____ _____ _____ _____

2. cello _____ _____ _____ _____

3. special _____ _____ _____ _____

4. homework _____ _____ _____ _____

5. heavy _____ _____ _____ _____

Week 21

A READ & SPELL

1. wrench
2. chain
3. drill
4. nail
5. hammer
6. perhaps
7. university
8. college
9. negative
10. positive

B COPY & SPELL

☑
☐ _____
☐ _____
☐ _____
☐ _____
☐ _____
☐ _____
☐ _____
☐ _____
☐ _____

C COVER & SPELL

_____
_____
_____
_____
_____
_____
_____
_____
_____

MYSTERY WORDS

1. I am a series of connected links often used in jewelry or for securing things. What am I? _____

2. I'm not positive. I'm the opposite. I might describe your mood if you hurt your foot. I am an electrical charge. What am I? _____

Fill in the blanks using the words below.
You will not use all of the words.

college	nail	university	negative	perhaps
hammer	positive	drill	chain	wrench

1. _____ we should go to the park tomorrow if the weather is nice.

2. Jacob used a strong _____ to lock his bike up outside.

3. The _____ was used to tighten the bolts on the bicycle.

4. My older sister is studying psychology at a _____ in New York.

5. Using a _____, he drove the nail into the wood to finish building the birdhouse.

6. It's important to keep a _____ attitude, even when things are tough.

7. Jane is considering applying to a community _____ after she graduates from high school.

8. He used a _____ to create a hole in the wall for the new electrical outlet.

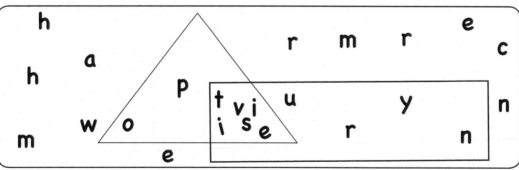

Look at the letters in the shapes and then answer the questions below

h
h   a
m   w   o
                    p
                 t v i u
                 i s e   y
                        r   n
r   m   r   e
                            c
                            n

1. **What word can you make with the letters in the triangle?**

   _____

2. **What word can you make with the letters in the rectangle?**

   _____

3. **What two words can you make with the letters outside both shapes?**

   _____   _____

CATEGORY CONNECTION

For each group of words below, choose a spelling word from this week that best fits in the same category.

1. screwdriver, pliers, saw _____

2. elementary school, middle school, high school _____

3. screw, bolt, rivet _____

4. yes, no, maybe _____

5. cogwheel, pulley, lever _____

6. Harvard, Stanford, Yale _____

7. smile, laugh, cheer _____

8. frown, cry, complain _____

9. sander, grinder, lathe _____

10. link, connection, bond _____

For each row of letters circle the 2nd letter, then the 4th letter, then the 6th letter, and so on. Write those circled letters on the first blank line to make a word. Now, write the letters you didn't circle on the second blank line. Finally, write both words again below, in your neatest cursive handwriting!

p n o e s g i a t t i i v v e e

1. _____
   _____
   _____
   _____

p h e a r m h m a e p r s

2. _____
   _____
   _____
   _____

d n r a i i l l l

3. _____
   _____
   _____
   _____

w c r h e a n i c n h

4. _____
   _____
   _____
   _____

These mice love to eat cheese!
1. Write the spelling words in alphabetical order on each piece of cheese.
2. Have fun coloring!

8

10

5

2

3

9

7

6

4

1

A) READ & SPELL

1. umbrella
2. Europe
3. subject
4. package
5. generalize
6. elevator
7. anything
8. ready
9. guest
10. hotel

B) COPY & SPELL

☑
☐ _____
☐ _____
☐ _____
☐ _____
☐ _____
☐ _____
☐ _____
☐ _____
☐ _____

C) COVER & SPELL

_____
_____
_____
_____
_____
_____
_____
_____
_____

MYSTERY WORDS

1. I start specific and make it broad. I turn one fact into a rule for all. What am I? _____

2. I'm not nothing, and I'm not something specific. I could be everything or just something. What am I? _____

Decode the words below and then unscramble them!

A	B	C	D	E	F	G	H	I	J	K	L	M

N	O	P	Q	R	S	T	U	V	W	X	Y	Z

1

2

3

_____

_____

4

5

6

_____

_____

7

8

_____

_____

9

10

_____

_____

With the spelling words from this week, fill in the blanks in the story below. Some words may be used twice!

In the exciting town of Zingaroo, there was a unique place where people stayed when they visited. It was an extraordinary _____ known for its enchanting surprises. One of the surprises was a friendly penguin named Pippin. Pippin loved to welcome every person who came to stay, each one a valued _____.

Pippin was always _____ to welcome new people, regardless of the weather. Even on rainy days, he was prepared, thanks to his magical _____ given to him by Mr. Cooper.

Mr. Cooper was a magical person who lived at the _____. He was known as the hotel's resident wizard and he brought the magical _____ back from his grand travels in a far-off continent called _____.

One sunny afternoon, Pippin noticed something interesting sitting at the front desk. It was a mysterious _____. Excited, Pippin waddled over to inspect it. The friendly person who worked at the front desk, called a bellhop, noticed Pippin's curiosity and decided to open the box. Inside, they found a small toy rowboat.

Suddenly the _____ made a noise, and when the door opened out stepped Mr. Cooper. Seeing the rowboat, he laughed and said, "Pippin, that rowboat reminds me of the time I rowed down the Seine River in France!"

The rowboat might have been just a toy, but to Pippin, it was a symbol of adventure. Inspired, Mr. Cooper decided to teach Pippin about his travels. He talked about the people he met, the cultures he experienced, and why it's important not to _____ or make assumptions about different places or people.

The day turned into another fun and educational experience for everyone.

WEEK 22

Use a spelling word from this week to complete each analogy below.

1.   **Specific** is to **focus** as **random** is to _____.

2.   **Home** is to **family** as **visitor** is to _____.

3.   **Prepare** is to **cook** as **train** is to _____.

4.   **Stairs** are to **walking** as **riding** is to _____.

5.   **Asia** is to **Japan** as **France** is to _____.

6.   **Class** is to **student** as **lesson** is to _____.

7.   **Detail** is to **specify** as **summary** is to _____.

8.   **Book** is to **cover** as **goods** is to _____.

9.   **Coat** is to **cold** as **rain** is to _____.

10. **Host** is to **party** as **invitee** is to _____.

Write the spelling words in alphabetical order on the igloo.
Have fun coloring!

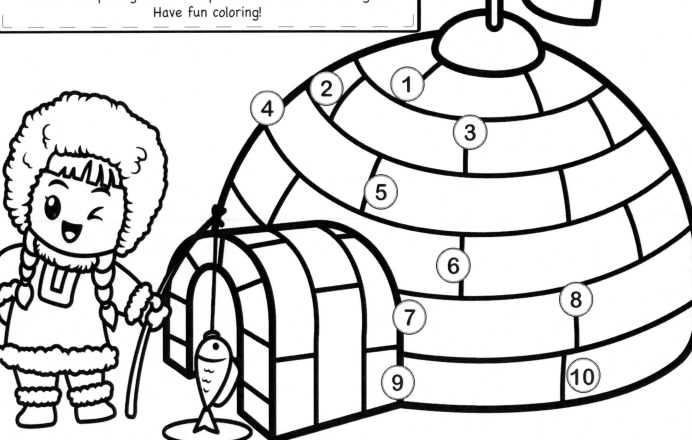

Week 23

A) READ & SPELL

1. region
2. return
3. believe
4. joined
5. member
6. contest
7. reject
8. Asia
9. unite
10. computer

B) COPY & SPELL

☑

☐ _____

☐ _____

☐ _____

☐ _____

☐ _____

☐ _____

☐ _____

☐ _____

☐ _____

C) COVER & SPELL

_____

_____

_____

_____

_____

_____

_____

_____

_____

MYSTERY WORDS

1. I'm a part of a whole, a section or piece. In geography and areas, I never cease. What am I? _____

2. I bring things together, even when they're apart. I make one from many, like a work of art. What am I? _____

Choose 5 spelling words then write a short story <u>in cursive or in print</u> using all the words. Check your grammar and punctuation. Be creative and have fun!

_____

_____

_____

_____

_____

_____

_____

_____

_____

Write a **SYNONYM** for each word below	Write an **ANTONYM** for each word below
1. region _____	**1.** return _____
2. return _____	**2.** believe _____
3. believe _____	**3.** joined _____
4. joined _____	**4.** member _____
5. member _____	**5.** contest _____
6. contest _____	**6.** reject _____
7. reject _____	**7.** unite _____
8. unite _____	
9. computer _____	

COLOR IN THE CIRCLES YOU NEED TO SPELL EACH WORD IN THE BOX. UNSCRAMBLE THE LEFTOVER CIRCLES TO SPELL A WORD FROM THIS WEEK.

WEEK 23

computer   contest   joined   reject   Asia   region   member

E I

B C T R E M V J J R O

R D R C E E M O P O

N E N O B E E G J O

C T S E I E M N I E

A I T U T E L S A

Write the hidden word here:

Which spelling word is most difficult?
Write it in a sentence to help you remember!

MASTERING DEFINITIONS THROUGH CURSIVE PRACTICE

Trace over each definition, then write it again below in cursive. Lastly, match each word with its correct definition by writing the word in cursive next to it.

region   return   believe   joined   member
contest   reject   Asia   unite   computer

1. _____ *to refuse to accept, consider, submit to, take for some purpose, or use*

   ----

2. _____ *one of the individuals composing a group*

   ----

3. _____ *to consider to be true or honest*

   ----

4. _____ *to go back or come back again*

   ----

5. _____ *to put or bring together so as to form a unit*

FUN WITH MNEMONICS!

1. Create a unique phrase for each spelling word below.
2. Every new word in the phrase will start with each letter of the spelling words below.
3. Use this phrase to remember how to spell the word.
4. Write a sentence using your mnemonic to help it stick.

Ex. Basin "Bats Always Sleep In Night".

1. Asia _____

_____

2. computer _____

_____

3. member _____

_____

4. region _____

_____

A READ & SPELL

1. eighty
2. sheriff
3. rodeo
4. exercise
5. wagon
6. train
7. Australia
8. saddle
9. calf
10. develop

B COPY & SPELL

☑
☐ _____
☐ _____
☐ _____
☐ _____
☐ _____
☐ _____
☐ _____
☐ _____
☐ _____

C COVER & SPELL

_____
_____
_____
_____
_____
_____
_____
_____
_____

MYSTERY WORDS

1. I rest on the back of a horse, a place to sit during the course.
   What am I? _____

2. I'm a routine you do for health, with jumping jacks, running, or stealth.
   What am I? _____

WEEK 24

This gorilla is the king sure does love eating pancakes! And he's hungry!
1. Write the spelling words in alphabetical order on each pancake.
2. Have fun coloring!

Circle each spelling word in the word search. Write each word twice in the blank spaces below as you find it.

```
                B  A
             T  K  V  U
          V  A  F  M  A  S
       J  F  Y  B  E  J  Y  T
       L  H  B  H  T  F  W  T  G  R
    H  A  F  G  S  B  H  A  O  N  D  A
    W  K  W  G  O  H  M  T  G  S  K  K  P  L
    B  C  B  K  N  F  E  G  L  O  I  R  D  F  H  I
    E  Q  A  E  D  L  Y  R  K  I  N  W  E  E  S  L  O  A
 J  V  S  L  L  X  O  X  I  N  K  W  E  R  V  I  O  U  P  V
 O  T  B  F  D  A  E  S  F  T  N  Q  X  T  E  E  I  J  Z  Q
    M  C  H  D  A  D  R  F  R  K  G  W  G  L  E  H  B  J
    B  R  A  R  O  D  C  A  I  E  Y  T  O  S  P  J
       C  S  P  R  L  I  I  H  X  C  G  P  T  A
       R  B  U  M  Q  N  S  O  M  T  H  G
       F  Y  N  R  K  X  E  P  U  Z
          G  L  Z  Z  M  U  N  J
          U  X  B  C  M  Q
             S  Q  H  P
             Z  V
```

 1 _____ _____

6 _____ _____

2 _____ _____

7 _____ _____

3 _____ _____

8 _____ _____

4 _____ _____

9 _____ _____

5 _____ _____

10 _____ _____

Fill in the crisscross puzzle boxes with two spelling words from this week that share the same letter. Then, write those words again underneath in your best <u>cursive</u> writing!

① e ☐ ☐ ☐ ☐ ☐ ☐

② ☐ ☐ ☐ r ☐ ☐ ☐

③ a ☐ ☐ ☐ ☐ ☐ ☐ ☐

④ ☐ a ☐ ☐ ☐

_____   _____

_____   _____

Circle the correctly spelled words.
Then rewrite the incorrect words on the lines to the right.

sadlle	sheriff	exurcise
train	eighty	wagun
calf	rodeo	develope

① _____

② _____

③ _____

④ _____

Week 25

A **READ & SPELL**

1. window
2. emerald
3. eighteen
4. heart
5. site
6. harbor
7. corner
8. barber
9. garlic
10. probably

B **COPY & SPELL**

☑

☐ _____

☐ _____

☐ _____

☐ _____

☐ _____

☐ _____

☐ _____

☐ _____

☐ _____

C **COVER & SPELL**

_____

_____

_____

_____

_____

_____

_____

_____

_____

MYSTERY WORDS

1. I'm a place where boats find rest, a safe and sheltered place that's best. What am I? _____

2. I'm a word used when you're not sure, but you think that something might occur. What am I? _____

**Fill in the blanks using the words below.
You will not use all of the words.**

| heart | emerald | eighteen | corner | barber |
| window | site | harbor | garlic | probably |

1. In cooking class, we learned how to peel and mince _____.

2. On my next birthday I will be turning _____.

3. The ship was safely anchored in the _____.

4. He got a new haircut from the _____ downtown.

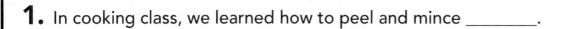

5. She wore an _____ necklace that sparkled in the light.

6. If we finish our chores quickly, we'll _____ have time to go to the park.

7. When you look out of the _____, you can see the beautiful mountains.

8. She placed her hand on her _____ when she got surprised.

Look at the letters in the shapes and then answer the questions below

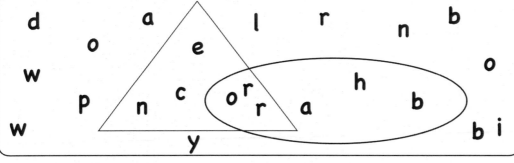

1. What word can you make with the letters in the triangle?

    _____

2. What word can you make with the letters in the oval?

    _____

3. What two words can you make with the letters outside both shapes?

    _____ _____

MASTERING DEFINITIONS THROUGH CURSIVE PRACTICE

Trace over each definition, then write it again below in cursive. Lastly, match each word with its correct definition by writing the word in cursive next to it.

site   heart   eighteen   emerald   window
harbor   corner   barber   garlic   probably

1. _____ one whose business is cutting and dressing hair, and related services

----

2. _____ a hollow muscle in vertebrates that pumps blood throughout the body

----

3. _____ the place, scene, or point of an occurrence or event

----

4. _____ the point where converging lines, edges, or sides meet

----

5. _____ an opening especially in the wall of a building to let in light and air

----

For each row of letters circle the 2nd letter, then the 4th letter, then the 6th letter, and so on. Write those circled letters on the first blank line to make a word. Now, write the letters you didn't circle on the second blank line. Finally, write both words again below, in your neatest cursive handwriting!

1   p e r i o g b h a t b e l e y n

2   e g m a e r r l a i l c d

3   c b o a r r n b e e r r

4   h w a i r n b d o o r w

WEEK 25

Decode the words below and then unscramble them!

A	B	C	D	E	F	G	H	I	J	K	L	M

N	O	P	Q	R	S	T	U	V	W	X	Y	Z

(1) _____ _____

(2) _____ _____

(3) _____ _____

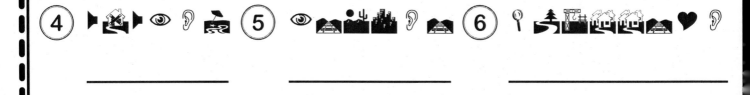

(4) _____ _____

(5) _____ _____

(6) _____ _____

(7) _____ _____

(8) _____ _____

(9) _____ _____

(10) _____ _____

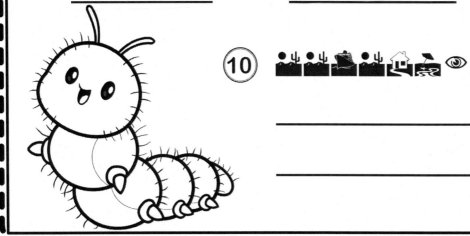

Ask a friend or family member choose any spelling words from this book and say them aloud. Test your memory and spelling skills by writing them down below!

Spelling Practice

1. _____

2. _____

3. _____

4. _____

5. _____

6. _____

7. _____

8. _____

9. _____

10. _____

Spelling Practice

1. _____

2. _____

3. _____

4. _____

5. _____

6. _____

7. _____

8. _____

9. _____

10. _____

Spelling Practice

1. _____

2. _____

3. _____

4. _____

5. _____

6. _____

7. _____

8. _____

9. _____

10. _____

Ask a friend or family member choose any spelling words from this book and say them aloud. Test your memory and spelling skills by writing them down below!

Spelling Practice

1. _____
2. _____
3. _____
4. _____
5. _____
6. _____
7. _____
8. _____
9. _____
10. _____

Spelling Practice

1. _____
2. _____
3. _____
4. _____
5. _____
6. _____
7. _____
8. _____
9. _____
10. _____

Spelling Practice

1. _____
2. _____
3. _____
4. _____
5. _____
6. _____
7. _____
8. _____
9. _____
10. _____

Ask a friend or family member choose any spelling words from this book and say them aloud. Test your memory and spelling skills by writing them down below!

Spelling Practice

1. _____
2. _____
3. _____
4. _____
5. _____
6. _____
7. _____
8. _____
9. _____
10. _____

Spelling Practice

1. _____
2. _____
3. _____
4. _____
5. _____
6. _____
7. _____
8. _____
9. _____
10. _____

Spelling Practice

1. _____
2. _____
3. _____
4. _____
5. _____
6. _____
7. _____
8. _____
9. _____
10. _____

Ask a friend or family member choose any spelling words from this book and say them aloud. Test your memory and spelling skills by writing them down below!

Spelling Practice

1. _____
2. _____
3. _____
4. _____
5. _____
6. _____
7. _____
8. _____
9. _____
10. _____

Spelling Practice

1. _____
2. _____
3. _____
4. _____
5. _____
6. _____
7. _____
8. _____
9. _____
10. _____

Spelling Practice

1. _____
2. _____
3. _____
4. _____
5. _____
6. _____
7. _____
8. _____
9. _____
10. _____

Could you spare just a minute?

Our biggest joy comes from helping little ones flourish and discover the world around them through learning.

That's why your thoughts matter so much to us!

Your honest thoughts about our book, even a quick sentence or two, would mean the world. We really mean it!

You'd be making a big difference for a small education brand like ours, run with love by a mother–daughter team.

Your reviews help us reach more curious minds across the globe, paving their way to success in their educational journey.

And hey, maybe we'll even sell a few more books in the process!

Every single review makes our hearts swell with gratitude.

Ready to make our day?

Scan the QR Code below to share your thoughts.

SCAN ME

Made in United States
North Haven, CT
17 January 2024

47605653R00061